ABDO
Publishing Company

MUSCULAR
System

BODY SYSTEMS

A Buddy Book by **Sarah Tieck**

Buddy **BOOKS**
Body Systems

VISIT US AT
www.abdopublishing.com

Published by ABDO Publishing Company, 8000 West 78th Street, Edina, Minnesota 55439.

Printed in the United States of America, North Mankato, Minnesota.
092010
012011

 PRINTED ON RECYCLED PAPER

Coordinating Series Editor: Rochelle Baltzer
Contributing Editors: Megan M. Gunderson, BreAnn Rumsch, Marcia Zappa
Graphic Design: Jenny Christensen
Cover Photograph: *iStockphoto*: ©iStockphoto.com/LUGO.
Interior Photographs/Illustrations: *Eighth Street Studio* (p. 22); *iStockphoto*: ©iStockphoto.
    com/ActionPics (p. 11), ©iStockphoto.com/bjones27 (p. 5), ©iStockphoto.com/bonniej
    (p. 13), ©iStockphoto.com/Eraxion (p. 19), ©iStockphoto.com/imagesbybarbara (p. 27),
    ©iStockphoto.com/jane (p. 25), ©iStockphoto.com/mpabild (p. 22), ©iStockphoto.com/
    RBFried (p. 17), ©iStockphoto.com/skynesher (p. 30); *Peter Arnold, Inc.*: Ed Reschke
    (p. 15); *Photo Researchers, Inc.*: BSIP (pp. 7, 17); *Shutterstock*: Computer Earth (p. 23),
    Andrea Danti (p. 21), Glen Jones (p. 25), Monkey Business Images (pp. 29, 30), Tyler
    Olson (p. 19), Sophie Louise Phelps (p. 23), photobank.kiev.ua (p. 9).

Library of Congress Cataloging-in-Publication Data

Tieck, Sarah, 1976-
  Muscular system / Sarah Tieck.
    p. cm. -- (Body systems)
  ISBN 978-1-61613-499-0
  1. Muscles--Juvenile literature. I. Title.
  QP321.T54 2011
  612.7'4--dc22
                        2010019664

Table of Contents

Amazing Body

Your body is amazing! It does thousands of things each day. Your body parts help you grow, run, and breathe.

Groups of body parts make up body systems. Each system does important work. The muscular system allows your body to move. Let's learn more about it!

Your muscular system works with every part of your body.

Working Together

Your muscular system is inside your body. It is made up of body **tissue** called muscle. The three types of muscle are skeletal, smooth, and cardiac.

Skeletal muscles support your bones and give your body shape. Smooth muscles make up your **organs**. Cardiac muscle is found in your heart.

6

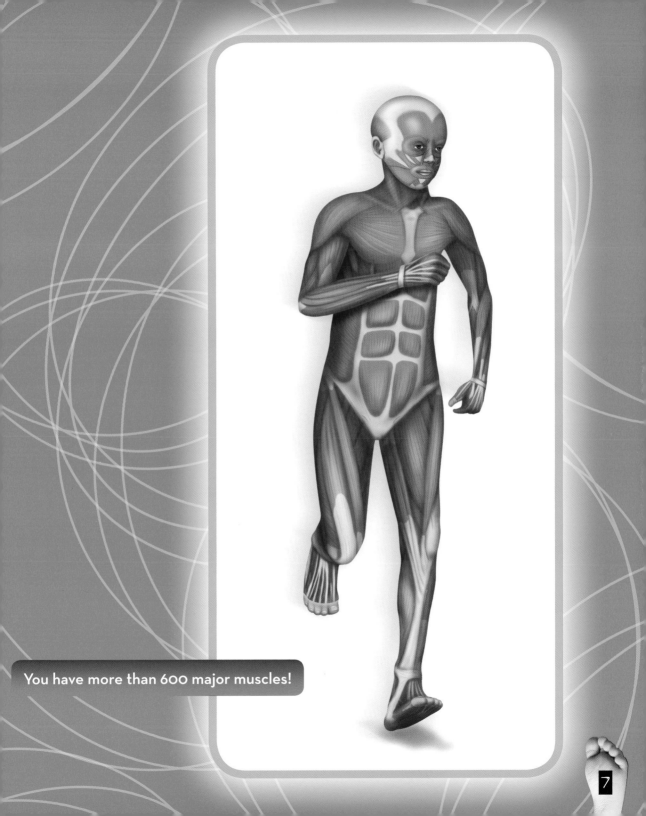

You have more than 600 major muscles!

On the Surface

Your skeletal muscles connect to your skeleton. They **stretch** across your bones and join them together. They pull on your bones to move your body.

Strong bands of **tissue** called tendons help your skeletal muscles. They connect your muscles to bones. Tendons work with muscles so you can move.

YOUR SKELETAL MUSCLES

Triceps

Biceps

Abdominal Muscles

Gluteus Maximus

Hamstring Muscles

Quadriceps

You can control your skeletal muscles. These muscles power your body to lift, turn, and walk. They can move your body in many different directions.

Many muscles work together for some movements. For example, your leg muscles allow you to walk. At the same time, your stomach and back muscles hold you up.

Your arms won't swing a baseball bat unless you tell them to!

Made to Move

A muscle consists of muscle fibers. These are long, thin cells made of **proteins**. One muscle contains many groups of muscle fibers.

Muscles move your body by contracting. This action makes the muscle fibers shorter. When muscles relax, they return to their original shape and size.

Your quadriceps and hamstring muscles are leg muscle groups that help you walk and kick.

In order to move, your skeletal muscles work with nerves. Nerves carry messages from your brain to your muscle fibers. These messages let your muscles know when to contract.

Up close, your skeletal muscles look like stripes. Can you see the nerves connected to the muscle fibers?

Support System

Skeletal muscles work in pairs. They have muscle partners that move in the opposite way.

For example, muscle partners move your arms. Your biceps are on the front of your upper arms. They pull your forearms up. Your triceps are on the back of your upper arms. They pull your forearms down.

Your triceps and biceps are at work when you dribble a basketball!

Biceps

Triceps

Smooth Muscles

Smooth muscles power your organs. These include your stomach, intestines, and lungs. Your skin has smooth muscles, too. Most smooth muscles look like sheets of tissue.

Unlike skeletal muscles, you cannot control smooth muscles. They work without you even thinking about it!

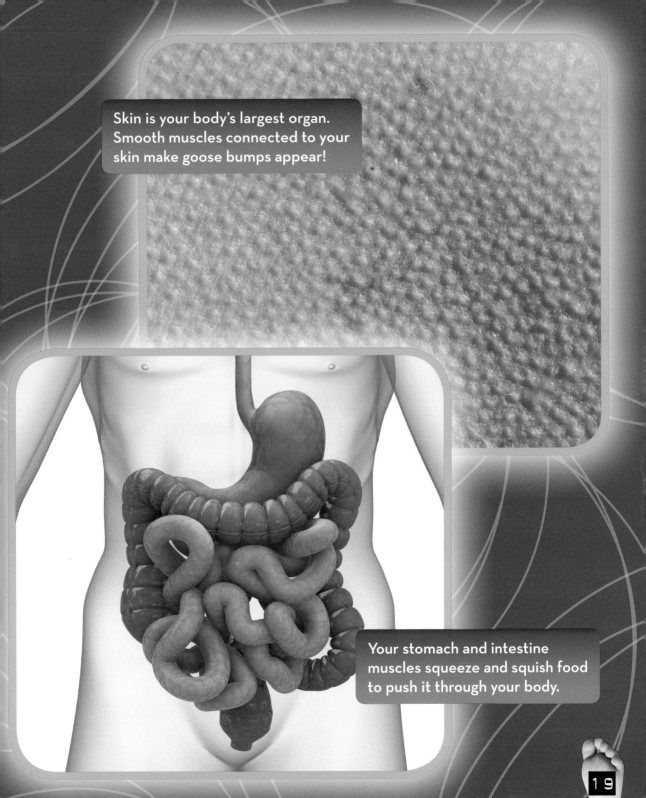

Skin is your body's largest organ. Smooth muscles connected to your skin make goose bumps appear!

Your stomach and intestine muscles squeeze and squish food to push it through your body.

19

At the Heart

Cardiac muscle makes up the walls of your heart. This muscle allows your heart to beat. It contracts to push out blood. It relaxes to let in blood. These movements make the sound of your heartbeat!

Inside your heart, a group of cells called the pacemaker sets your heart rate. If it becomes unhealthy, a man-made pacemaker can replace it.

WORD OF MOUTH

Your heart beats to keep you alive. Keep it strong by exercising your body!

Brain Food

What is your hardest-working muscle?

Many would say it is your heart. It beats your whole life without stopping! Usually, it beats 60 to 100 times per minute. It moves even faster when you exercise.

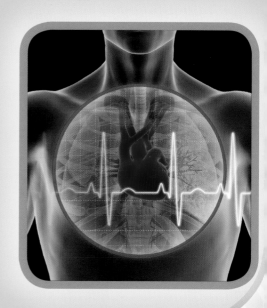

What is a six pack?

This is a way of saying someone has strong abdominal muscles. You can often see how strong they are. Six-pack abs bulge in six different places!

What are some of your busiest muscles?

Your eye muscles are busy. They move about 100,000 times each day!

A tendon in your heel is named for the ancient Greek soldier Achilles. In a story, he died after his heel was hit by an arrow.

Push and Pull

Activities and accidents are common causes of **injured** muscles. For example, you might tear a muscle or a tendon while playing a sport.

Often when your muscles are hurt, you can help them heal. Be sure to get plenty of rest. Using ice packs can also ease your pain.

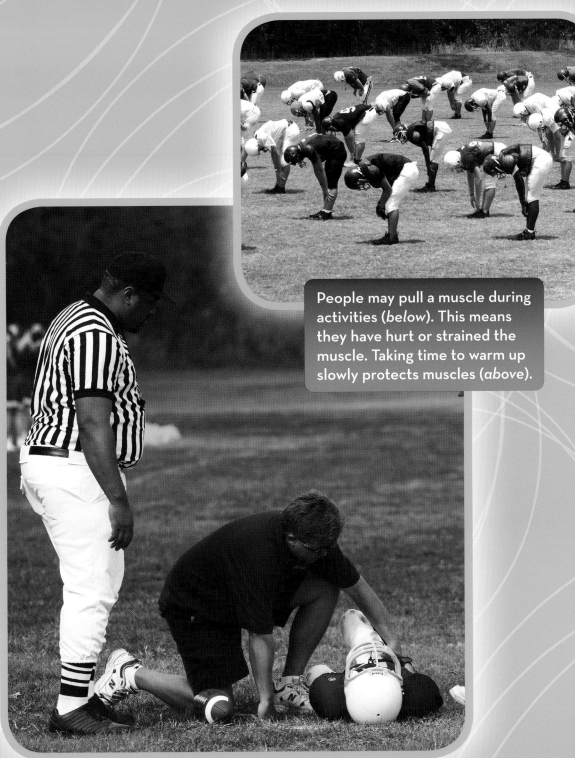

People may pull a muscle during activities (*below*). This means they have hurt or strained the muscle. Taking time to warm up slowly protects muscles (*above*).

Sharp, lasting pain or trouble moving are signs of serious muscle problems. Some illnesses can weaken muscles.

For serious problems, people need to see doctors. Doctors have tools to check muscles. They also have ways to slow or stop muscle illnesses.

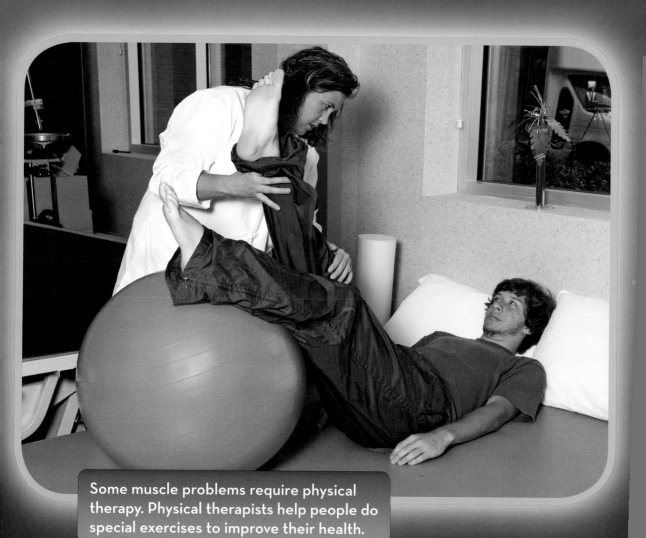

Some muscle problems require physical therapy. Physical therapists help people do special exercises to improve their health.

An Important System

Think about how much you can do because of your muscles! By learning about your muscular system, you can **protect** it. Then, you can make good choices to keep your body healthy.

Stay active to keep your muscles strong!

HEALTHY BODY FILES

WORK IT

✔ Your skeletal muscles get stronger when you lift weights. Activities such as walking, running, and swimming also strengthen them.

✔ Exercise strengthens your cardiac muscle, too.

STAY SAFE

✔ Take time to warm up before a hard workout. This helps keep your muscles from getting injured.

GET FIT

✔ Your muscles need vitamins and minerals to grow strong. Fruits and vegetables contain lots of these.

✔ Protein is good fuel for strong muscles. Meat, cheese, eggs, milk, and fish contain lots of protein.

Important Words

injure (IHN-juhr) to cause pain or harm.

organ a body part that does a special job. The heart and the lungs are organs.

protect (pruh-TEHKT) to guard against harm or danger.

protein (PROH-teen) an important part of the diet of all animals.

stretch to spread out to full size or greater.

tissue (TIH-shoo) a group of cells that form a part of a living thing.

Web Sites

To learn more about the muscular system, visit ABDO Publishing Company online. Web sites about the muscular system are featured on our Book Links page. These links are routinely monitored and updated to provide the most current information available.

www.abdopublishing.com

Index